An Imprint of Pop!
popbooksonline.com

The Eras of Taylor Swift

# THE EVERMORE era

## Track List

1. willow
2. champagne problems
3. gold rush
4. 'tis the d— season
5. tolerate it
6. no body, no crime (ft. HAIM)
7. happiness
8. dorothea
9. coney island (ft. The National)
10. ivy
11. cowboy like me
12. long story short
13. marjorie
14. closure
15. evermore (ft. Bon Iver)

by Elizabeth Andrews

# WELCOME TO DiscoverRoo!

This book is filled with videos, puzzles, games, and more! Scan the QR codes* while you read, or visit the website below to make this book pop.

popbooksonline.com/Evermore

**abdobooks.com**

Published by Pop!, a division of ABDO, PO Box 398166, Minneapolis, Minnesota 55439. 

Printed in the United States of America, North Mankato, Minnesota.

082025
012026

THIS BOOK CONTAINS RECYCLED MATERIALS

Cover Photo: Alexandra Tarasova (BigArtLab); Shutterstock Images

Interior Photos: Capital Pictures/Alamy; Getty Images; Invision/AP; PaoloV/Flickr; Shutterstock Images; SIPAUSA/AP; SIPAUSA/Alamy

Editors: Grace Hansen and Anna Schwartz

Series Designer: Laura Graphenteen

**Library of Congress Control Number: 2025941002**

**Publisher's Cataloging-in-Publication Data**

Names: Andrews, Elizabeth, author.

Title: The Evermore era / by Elizabeth Andrews

Description: Minneapolis, Minnesota : Pop!, 2026 | Series: The eras of Taylor Swift | Includes online resources and index

Identifiers: ISBN 9781098248680 (lib. bdg.) | ISBN 9781098249205 (ebook)

Subjects: LCSH: Swift, Taylor, 1989- --Juvenile literature. | Popular music--Juvenile literature. | Popular (Songs, etc.)--Juvenile literature. | Albums--Juvenile literature. | Concerts--Juvenile literature. | Mass media and music--Juvenile literature.

Classification: DDC 782.42164093--dc23

*Scanning QR codes requires a web-enabled smart device with a QR code reader app and a camera.

# TABLE OF CONTENTS

CHAPTER 1

# FOLLOW THE STRING

On December 10, 2020, Taylor Swift took to Twitter (now X) and Instagram to surprise her fans. A new album would once again drop at midnight. She posted nine photos on her Instagram. The nine posts fit together like a puzzle on the grid and formed the cover image for *evermore*.

WATCH A VIDEO HERE!

# Meet Taylor

Birthday: December 13, 1989
Star Sign: Sagittarius
Place of Birth: West Reading, PA
Favorite Number: 13
Favorite Color: Purple
Favorite Food: Chicken tenders and a chocolate shake

13

Benjamin Button

XOXO

Olivia Benson

Taylor Swift

Only five months had passed since Taylor dropped her first surprise album, *folklore,* in the same way. Taylor said the album was a gift for fans. It was a point of joy and excitement as people were preparing for a lonely holiday season during the COVID-19 **pandemic**.

*Taylor likely took photos for* Red (Taylor's Version) *while she posed for* evermore's *album art.*

**DID YOU KNOW?**

Taylor was also rerecording *Fearless* when she was putting *evermore* together.

At midnight on December 11, *evermore* was released. Fans did not have the chance to imagine what the album would be like. There was no **single** released before the album to **inspect** for clues. All at once, there were 15 brand new tracks that seemed to connect with the album that came before.

## ALBUMS WITHOUT EXPECTATIONS

In her past, Taylor kept a routine of writing an album, releasing it, and then planning and performing a world tour. *Folklore* and *evermore* were the first time Taylor could write an album simply to create art. She took away the pressure of making things bigger and better. The freedom she found while writing let her explore new ways to make music.

The first single off *evermore* was "willow." Taylor released the music video for it at the same time the album dropped. In the music video, Taylor follows a golden string through different worlds and finds her fated love. This song has many Easter eggs connecting it to *folklore*. Easter eggs are clues and secret messages Taylor hides in her work. The video opens where the music video for "cardigan" left off. She also returns to the *folklore* cabin at the end of the song.

## Easter Egg

"Cardigan" and "willow" both mention scars in their lyrics. She also writes about scars in *Taylor Swift*, *1989*, *Lover*, and *The Tortured Poets Department*.

*The golden string Taylor follows in the "willow" video is likely a reference to another folklore song, "invisible string."*

CHAPTER 2

# A SISTER

Taylor made *evermore* with Aaron Dessner and Jack Antonoff. They are the same **producers** that worked on *folklore*. After finishing *folklore*, Taylor and Aaron couldn't stop writing music. She said she felt "like [they] were standing on the edge

EXPLORE LINKS HERE!

of the folklorian woods and had a choice: to turn and go back or to travel further into the forest of this music."

*Aaron Dessner (center) plays in The National. Jack Antonoff (left) plays in Bleachers.*

*Taylor got much of her inspiration for evermore from the movies and books she was watching and reading at the time.*

Taylor said that *evermore* is a sister album to *folklore*. She saw *folklore* as spring and summer. She wanted to fill in the rest of the year. Taylor sees *evermore* as fall and winter. *Evermore* doesn't exactly continue the stories from the album before it, but it has strings that connect to them.

Unlike most of Taylor's previous albums, which are **autobiographical**, *evermore* is an album full of others' stories. Taylor said there are 17 new tales on *evermore*. Some of the stories are about two young **con artists** who fall in love, college sweethearts, and marriages that did not result in happily ever after. Taylor's grandma Marjorie also gets her own song.

*Marjorie Finlay won a television talent contest called* Music With the Girls.

CHAPTER 3

# STORY ENDINGS

One theme that carries through *evermore* is endings. The songs on the album tell the tales of the end of a relationship, the end of a friendship, the end of something **toxic**, and all the pain that comes with endings. The stories are most likely fiction, but Taylor has said she weaves her own emotions and experiences into the music.

COMPLETE AN ACTIVITY HERE!

Taylor wrote some songs with her boyfriend at the time, Joe Alwyn. He wrote under the name William Bowery.

*Joe and Taylor wrote songs based on piano pieces he put together during COVID-19.*

“Champagne problems” is a very sad song Taylor co-wrote with Joe Alwyn. They both love sad songs. Taylor said the song is about “longtime college sweethearts [who] had very different plans for the same night, one to end it and one who brought a ring.” She loves the **bridge** in this song and was excited to sing it in front of a crowd.

"Dorothea" is about a girl who leaves her small town to chase her dreams of becoming a Hollywood star. She left her boyfriend behind. The song is from her ex's perspective now that she made it big. He wants her to know he'll always be there if she ever comes home.

**DID YOU KNOW?**

Many people believe Dorothea is based on Taylor's good friend Selena Gomez.

"'Tis the d— season" is likely another song about Dorothea. This time it is from her perspective. Dorothea goes home for a weekend after chasing her dreams and knows she will run into her old love. If they meet up, it could be comfortable and dreamy. But it would only be for the weekend, not forever.

*On nights that HAIM performed on the Eras Tour, Taylor sang "no body, no crime" instead of "'tis the d— season."*

*Taylor is close friends with all three Haim sisters. They were featured on the song "no body, no crime."*

Marjorie was Taylor's grandma on her mother's side.

"Marjorie" is track 13 on *evermore*. Taylor's favorite number is 13, so songs in that spot on the track list hold a special place in her heart. "Marjorie" is named after Taylor's grandmother. She was an opera singer. The song holds advice from Marjorie. You can even hear her singing opera in the background. This song is about Taylor feeling like her grandma is still with her and guiding her through life.

CHAPTER 4

# LEAVING THE WOODS

"Evermore" is the final song on the album. Taylor wrote and performed it with Bon Iver. She is a huge fan of his. They wrote this song during a stressful time in the United States. The song follows a

Emily Dickinson

LEARN MORE HERE!

*Most of evermore was recorded at Long Pond Studio in Hudson Valley, New York.*

path through a forest as months pass. Things are cold and uncertain. Finally, the person in the song finds a warm, cozy cabin to stay in. Taylor wanted to end the album with this feeling.

## Easter Egg

The album name, *evermore*, might be connected to the poet Emily Dickinson. She ended one of her most romantic poems with "forevermore." Some Swifties think "ivy" is about Dickinson.

*Taylor's producer Aaron Dessner connected her with Bon Iver.*

Even though "evermore" was a perfect way to end, Taylor had two more songs up her sleeve for the deluxe version. "Right where you left me" is about a girl who stays frozen forever where her heart was broken. "It's time to go" is about trusting your gut when it tells you to get out of a situation. Many people think it is about Taylor's old **label** not giving her the rights to her own music.

*Taylor was in charge of her own hair, makeup, and styling for evermore's album art.*

*The glowing balls held by the dancers during the* evermore *set are also seen in the "willow" music video.*

When the Eras Tour began, *evermore* had its own set. The screen showed a moody forest, and pine trees grew from the stage. Taylor and her dancers performed a witchy routine for "willow." When she sang "marjorie," a large oak

tree grew. During “tolerate it,” Taylor sang at a long table set for two. After *The Tortured Poets Department* was added to the tour, *folklore* and *evermore* were combined. Elements from each set were still used after Taylor put them together.

*Taylor wore only two different* evermore *dresses during the Eras Tour, a yellow one and a sparkly bronze one.*

*Evermore* did not make as big of a splash on the awards scene as *folklore* did. Since the albums were released in the same year, that was to be expected. Still, *evermore* won the American Music Award for Favorite Pop Album. It was also nominated for Album of the Year at the 64th **Grammy Awards**.

*Taylor had to accept many awards for evermore from home because of COVID-19 restrictions.*

# MAKING CONNECTIONS

## TEXT-TO-SELF

What is your favorite song from the *Evermore* Era? Why is it your favorite?

## TEXT-TO-TEXT

Have you read books about any other music artists? How are they similar to or different from Taylor Swift?

## TEXT-TO-WORLD

As a reader, why do you think so many people around the world connect with Taylor Swift and her music? Write a few sentences to explain your answer.

# GLOSSARY

**autobiographical** — relating to a person's own life and experience.

**bridge** — a section in the middle of a song that is clearly different from the other parts.

**con artist** — a person who tricks others.

**Grammy Awards** — an event that recognizes and awards remarkable works in music throughout the year.

**inspect** — to look very carefully.

**label** — a company that helps make and release music recordings.

**pandemic** — an outbreak of a disease that spreads across a large area.

**producer** — someone who organizes the creation of music recordings.

**single** — a song that is released as a stand-alone from the album.

**toxic** — acting like a poison.

# INDEX

DiscoverRoo!
ONLINE RESOURCES

This book is filled with videos, puzzles, games, and more! Scan the QR codes* while you read, or visit the website below to make this book pop.

popbooksonline.com/Evermore

*Scanning QR codes requires a web-enabled smart device with a QR code reader app and a camera.